Common Core Language Arts Workouts Grade 6

AUTHOR: Linda Armstrong
EDITORS: Mary Dieterich and Sarah M. Anderson
PROOFREADER: Margaret Brown

COPYRIGHT © 2015 Mark Twain Media, Inc.

ISBN 978-1-62223-522-3

Printing No. CD-404226

Mark Twain Media, Inc., Publishers
Distributed by Carson-Dellosa Publishing LLC

Table of Contents
With Common Core State Standards Correlations

    CCSS.ELA-Literacy.RL.6.1: Cite textual evidence to support analysis of what the text says explicitly as well as inferences drawn from the text.

    CCSS.ELA-Literacy.RL.6.2: Determine a theme or central idea of a text and how it is conveyed through particular details; provide a summary of the text distinct from personal opinions or judgments.

    CCSS.ELA-Literacy.RL.6.3: Describe how a particular story's or drama's plot unfolds in a series of episodes as well as how the characters respond or change as the plot moves toward a resolution.

    CCSS.ELA-Literacy.RL.6.4: Determine the meaning of words and phrases as they are used in a text, including figurative and connotative meanings; analyze the impact of a specific word choice on meaning and tone.

    CCSS.ELA-Literacy.RL.6.5: Analyze how a particular sentence, chapter, scene, or stanza fits into the overall structure of a text and contributes to the development of the theme, setting, or plot.

    CCSS.ELA-Literacy.RL.6.6: Explain how an author develops the point of view of the narrator or speaker in a text.

    CCSS.ELA-Literacy.RL.6.7: Compare and contrast the experience of reading a story, drama, or poem to listening to or viewing an audio, video, or live version of the text, including contrasting what they "see" and "hear" when reading the text to what they perceive when they listen or watch.

    CCSS.ELA-Literacy.RL.6.9: Compare and contrast texts in different forms or genres (e.g., stories and poems; historical novels and fantasy stories) in terms of their approaches to similar themes and topics.

    CCSS.ELA-Literacy.RI.6.1: Cite textual evidence to support analysis of what the text says explicitly as well as inferences drawn from the text.

    CCSS.ELA-Literacy.RI.6.2: Determine a central idea of a text and how it is conveyed through particular details; provide a summary of the text distinct from personal opinions or judgments.

    CCSS.ELA-Literacy.RI.6.3: Analyze in detail how a key individual, event, or idea is introduced, illustrated, and elaborated in a text (e.g., through examples or anecdotes).

    CCSS.ELA-Literacy.RI.6.4: Determine the meaning of words and phrases as they are used in a text, including figurative, connotative, and technical meanings.

    CCSS.ELA-Literacy.RI.6.5: Analyze how a particular sentence, paragraph, chapter, or section fits into the overall structure of a text and contributes to the development of the ideas.

Table of Contents
With Common Core State Standards Correlations (cont.)

Table of Contents
With Common Core State Standards Correlations (cont.)

Table of Contents
With Common Core State Standards Correlations (cont.)

Table of Contents
With Common Core State Standards Correlations (cont.)

Table of Contents
With Common Core State Standards Correlations (cont.)

* Skills and understandings that are particularly likely to require continued attention in higher grades as they are applied to increasingly sophisticated writing and speaking are marked with an asterisk (*).

Introduction to the Teacher

The time has come to make our children's reading, writing, and speaking education more rigorous. The Common Core State Standards were developed for this purpose. They guide educators and parents by outlining the skills students are expected to master at each grade level. The bar has been set high, but with a little help, students can meet the challenge.

Common Core Language Arts Workouts, Grade 6 is designed to assist teachers and parents who are implementing the new requirements. It is filled with skills practice pages, critical-thinking tasks, and creative exercises that correspond to each standard for language arts.

Each day, students will work with a different grade-level-specific language arts skill. The brief exercises will challenge them to read, think, and speak with improved facility.

Every page contains at least one "workout." The workouts vary according to the standard covered. Some are simple practice exercises. Others pose creative or analytical challenges. Certain pages invite further exploration. Suggested student projects include reports, speeches, discussions, and multimedia presentations.

The workout pages make great warm-up or assessment exercises. They can set the stage and teach the content covered by the standards. They can also be used to assess what students have learned after the content has been taught.

We hope that the ideas and exercises in this book will help you work more effectively with the Common Core State Standards. The series continues with books for Grade 7 and Grade 8. With your help, we are confident that students will develop increased language arts power and become more effective communicators!

Name: _____ Date: _____

READING LITERATURE – Between the Lines

CCSS.ELA-Literacy.RL.6.1: Cite textual evidence to support analysis of what the text says explicitly as well as inferences drawn from the text.

Directions: Read the passage and answer the questions that follow.

> Shadows deepened on barren cliffs across the valley. Mike gazed out the window across the vacant runway. Then, exasperated, he glanced at his cell phone, grimacing and shaking his head. He was certain to miss his connection. He considered returning to the coffee shop for a sandwich, but rejected the idea.

1. What time of day is it? How can you tell? _____

   _____

   _____

2. Mike is in a building. What kind of building is it? Which details tell you this? _____

   _____

   _____

3. How does he feel? Which words and phrases tell you this? _____

   _____

   _____

4. Is this building probably in a big city or a rural area? What information in the text leads you to believe this?

   _____

   _____

   _____

   _____

   _____

Name: _____ Date: _____

READING LITERATURE – What Is the Story About?

CCSS.ELA-Literacy.RL.6.2: Determine a theme or central idea of a text and how it is conveyed through particular details; provide a summary of the text distinct from personal opinions or judgments.

Directions: Read the passage and answer the questions that follow.

> The little boat pitched and rolled on the turbulent sea. Daniel watched helplessly as his father and the other divers struggled to hold it on a steady course against the ferocious storm. He wanted to help, but every time he tried to stand, pain seared through his leg.

1. Which of the following themes best fits this passage: materialism and downfall, greed, the power of wealth, man against nature, the power of names, or the power of words?

   _____

2. Which details in the passage support the theme? _____

   _____

   _____

3. What is the setting of the passage? How does it contribute to the theme? _____

   _____

   _____

4. Who is the main character? What is his problem? How does his problem relate to the theme?

   _____

   _____

   _____

   _____

CCSS.ELA-Literacy.RL.6.3 Describe how a particular story's or drama's plot unfolds in a series of episodes as well as how the characters respond or change as the plot moves toward a resolution.

Directions: On another sheet of paper, name a story, book, movie, or television show with a similar theme to the one in the passage above. Summarize the plot by telling how the main character solves his problems. Include the story's most important events.

Name: _____ Date: _____

READING LITERATURE – Power Words

CCSS.ELA-Literacy.RL.6.4: Determine the meaning of words and phrases as they are used in a text, including figurative and connotative meanings; analyze the impact of a specific word choice on meaning and tone.

Directions: Read the passage and answer the questions that follow.

> The graveyard was as desolate as space beyond the Kuiper Belt. Ancient granite markers loomed out of early-morning ground fog like primeval mountains in one of his grandfather's ink and wash paintings on rice paper. Lo Chi shifted the heavy backpack to his opposite shoulder. Lin was not really in that dismal place. She couldn't be. Only last week, her radiant smile had been as unsullied as the peonies in the garden at The Center.

1. The narrator tells us that the graveyard is as empty as something. What? What does this comparison tell us about the narrator?

   _____

   _____

   _____

2. What does *loomed* mean in this passage? What other words could have been used? How does *loomed* contribute to the mood of the selection?

   _____

   _____

   _____

3. What are the grave markers compared to? What does this tell you about the narrator? What might a mechanic, a computer technician, or other professional have compared them to?

   _____

   _____

   _____

4. Which two words in this passage describe something that is old? Which two words mean that something is sad? Why are these words used instead of their simpler equivalents?

   _____

   _____

   _____

Name: _____ Date: _____

READING LITERATURE – Supporting Roles

CCSS.ELA-Literacy.RL.6.5: Analyze how a particular sentence, chapter, scene, or stanza fits into the overall structure of a text and contributes to the development of the theme, setting, or plot.

Directions: Read the passage and answer the questions that follow.

> Jason cringed when he noticed Becca and Shawn alone together. They were standing in the shade of a eucalyptus tree on the periphery of the playground. They were definitely too close together for Jason's comfort. He didn't understand why this disturbed him so deeply. After all, he didn't like Becca that way, or did he?

1. What does the first sentence of this passage tell you about Jason and Becca? What does *cringed* mean? Why is it important in this sentence?

   _____

   _____

   _____

   _____

2. Which theme best describes this selection: vanity, first love, self-preservation, or an individual vs. society? Which sentence in the text most strongly supports the theme?

   _____

   _____

   _____

3. Which sentence tells you where this passage takes place? What does it tell you about the time and the weather?

   _____

   _____

   _____

4. Which sentence introduces the characters? Who is the point-of-view character? How do you know?

   _____

   _____

   _____

Name: _____ Date: _____

READING LITERATURE – Through Arlen's Eyes: Developing a Point of View

CCSS.ELA-Literacy.RL.6.6: Explain how an author develops the point of view of the narrator or speaker in a text.

Directions: Read the passage and answer the questions that follow.

> Arlen secured the thick door to his sleeping quarters, but he could still hear the two of them fighting downstairs. Their words were slurred and punctuated by fixtures crashing against the ship's unforgiving walls. Once, the older female called out his name, but he didn't respond. He had learned long before that interacting with either of them was pointless when they had drunk too much. If only his parents were still alive.

1. Who is the main character? _____

2. What is his problem? _____

   _____

3. How does he feel about his situation? _____

   _____

   _____

4. How would the selection be different if told from the point of view of one of the other characters?

   _____

   _____

   _____

CCSS.ELA-Literacy.RL.6.7: Compare and contrast the experience of reading a story, drama, or poem to listening to or viewing an audio, video, or live version of the text, including contrasting what they "see" and "hear" when reading the text to what they perceive when they listen or watch.

Directions: Which is better, reading a story or watching a film? Write your answer on another paper, using specific details and examples to support your opinion.

CCSS.ELA-Literacy.RL.6.9: Compare and contrast texts in different forms or genres (e.g., stories and poems; historical novels and fantasy stories) in terms of their approaches to similar themes and topics.

Directions: Read the short story "The Door" by E.B. White and the poem "Jabberwocky" by Lewis Carroll. (Both are available online.) How are they similar? How are they different? Write your answer on another sheet of paper.

Name: _____ Date: _____

READING INFORMATIONAL TEXT – Just the Facts

CCSS.ELA-Literacy.RI.6.1: Cite textual evidence to support analysis of what the text says explicitly as well as inferences drawn from the text.

Directions: Read the passage and answer the questions that follow.

A cell is the smallest unit of life. Every human body contains thousands of them, specialized for different tasks. However, many organisms have only one cell. That simple cell eats, eliminates waste, moves, and reproduces. One clear, blob-like type of single-celled creature probably lives near you. These tiny protists, called amoebas, thrive in lakes, ponds, puddles, and creeks. You can't see amoebas with your naked eye or an ordinary magnifying glass because they are too small. That doesn't stop mussels and water fleas from depending on them as a food source.

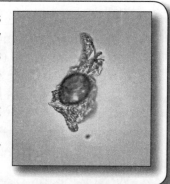

1. What do amoebas look like? _____

_____

_____

2. Name four places where amoebas may be found. What do those places have in common? What place do amoebas hold in the food web?

_____

_____

_____

_____

3. What tasks does the single-celled body of an amoeba perform? _____

_____

_____

4. What scientific tool might you use to see an amoeba? Which phrases in the selection lead you to infer this?

_____

_____

_____

Name: _____ Date: _____

READING INFORMATIONAL TEXT – How Details Add Up: Writing a Summary

CCSS.ELA-Literacy.RI.6.2: Determine a central idea of a text and how it is conveyed through particular details; provide a summary of the text distinct from personal opinions or judgments.

Directions: Read the passage and answer the questions that follow.

> For centuries, great European artists tried to make their paintings look real. They used linear perspective to give their pictures depth. They applied their knowledge of anatomy to make portraits more lifelike. Masters also studied light, shadow, and color. They used their observations to create illusions. These skilled painters could suggest subtle textures such as velvet, lace, silver, and glass.

1. What is the main idea of this selection? _____

_____

2. Why did artists use linear perspective? _____

_____

3. Why did European artists study anatomy? _____

_____

4. Why did they study light, shadow, and color? _____

_____

_____

CCSS.ELA-Literacy.RI.6.3: Analyze in detail how a key individual, event, or idea is introduced, illustrated, and elaborated in a text (e.g., through examples or anecdotes).

Directions: Read an article about your favorite artist, writer, or musician online or in a magazine. On your own paper, explain how the author of the article introduced the person. Then summarize the most important stories and facts the writer includes. Is the article presented in chronological order, or does it use some other text structure? Is it divided into sections? Does it include illustrations or charts? Share your observations with other members of your group.

Name: _____ Date: _____

READING INFORMATIONAL TEXT – The Clownfish and the Anemone: Using Context Clues

CCSS.ELA-Literacy.RI.6.4: Determine the meaning of words and phrases as they are used in a text, including figurative, connotative, and technical meanings.

Directions: Read the passage and answer the questions that follow.

Sometimes one organism needs another to live. This is called a symbiotic relationship. Some, called parasites, use others. For example, a clump of mistletoe extracts its food from the branch of a tree. Bacteria are small enough to live inside their host plants or animals. Mutualism is a different kind of symbiosis. The clownfish and a kind of sea anemone have this sort of arrangement. They help each other keep enemies away.

1. What does *symbiotic* mean? _____

   _____

   _____

2. What does *extracts* mean in this passage? _____

   _____

3. What are parasites? _____

   _____

   _____

4. What does *mutual* mean? How is the relationship between the clownfish and anemone different from the relationship between mistletoe and a tree or bacteria and an animal host?

   _____

   _____

   _____

   _____

Name: _____   Date: _____

READING INFORMATIONAL TEXT – One Small Step:
What Each Part of a Text Contributes

CCSS.ELA-Literacy.RI.6.5: Analyze how a particular sentence, paragraph, chapter, or section fits into the overall structure of a text and contributes to the development of the ideas.

Directions: Read the passage and answer the questions that follow.

> The year was 1969. Technology was simpler for most people. For example, there were no cell phones, personal computers, or digital cameras. In fact, many families still had black and white televisions. On the afternoon of July 20, all eyes were on Neil Armstrong. He was climbing down a ladder. The event was exciting because that ladder was a quarter of a million miles away. He was about to become the first human to set foot on the moon.

1. How does the fact that there were no cell phones, personal computers, or digital cameras describe life in 1969?

   _____

   _____

2. Why did the author add that many people still had black and white televisions?

   _____

3. How does the author describe what many people were doing on July 20, 1969?

   _____

4. What is the main idea of this selection? _____

   _____

5. Common signal terms for descriptive texts include *to illustrate, in addition, in fact, also, such as,* and *for example.* Which ones are used in this selection?

   _____

Directions: Read the transcript of the actual video transmission from Apollo 11 at <http://www.hq.nasa.gov/alsj/a11/a11.step.html>.

6. Which text structure best describes the way information is presented in the transcript?

   a. comparison and contrast   b. sequence

   c. description   d. cause and effect

   e. problem and solution

Name: _____ Date: _____

READING INFORMATIONAL TEXT – Abuzz With a Point of View: Determining the Author's Purpose

CCSS.ELA-Literacy.RI.6.6: Determine an author's point of view or purpose in a text and explain how it is conveyed in the text.

Directions: Read the passage and answer the questions that follow.

There's a bumblebee disaster brewing in North America. Since the late 1990s, their numbers have been declining alarmingly. Some species have almost disappeared. These insects pollinate more than a third of the foods people eat. We must act to save them before it is too late. Study the situation to find out what you can do.

1. What problem does the author discuss in this selection? _____

_____

_____

2. Is the author's purpose to entertain, inform, or persuade? How does the author convey this purpose in the passage?

_____

_____

_____

3. Which facts does the author include to show that the problem is important?

_____

_____

_____

4. What does the author want the reader to do? _____

_____

_____

Name: _____   Date: _____

READING INFORMATIONAL TEXT – A Picture is Worth a Thousand Words

CCSS.ELA-Literacy.RI.6.7: Integrate information presented in different media or formats (e.g., visually, quantitatively) as well as in words to develop a coherent understanding of a topic or issue.

Directions: Read the passage and the chart below. Then answer the questions that follow.

Giant Rock is a huge boulder. Located in the Mojave Desert, it might be the largest free-standing rock in the world. It is not surprising that this strange object is the subject of legends. Local Native Americans consider it sacred. In the 1950s, it drew thousands of believers in Unidentified Flying Objects (UFOs). In the year 2000, a piece as big as a truck broke off. Today, volunteers are working to pick up trash, remove graffiti, and protect this natural wonder from vandalism.

Giant Rock Facts

Location:	near Landers, California
Composition:	white granite
Height:	approximately 70 feet
Size at Base:	5,800 square feet (540 square meters)
Estimated weight:	more than 25,000 tons

1. What is Giant Rock and why are some people interested in it? _____

_____

_____

2. What information is shown in the picture that is not included in the text?

_____

_____

3. What information is included in the chart that is neither in the text nor the photograph?

_____

4. How does each type of media help readers understand Giant Rock? What other types of media could add important information?

_____

_____

Name: _____ Date: _____

READING INFORMATIONAL TEXT – Prove It!

CCSS.ELA-Literacy.RI.6.8: Trace and evaluate the argument and specific claims in a text, distinguishing claims that are supported by reasons and evidence from claims that are not.

Directions: Read the passage and answer the questions that follow.

> Bram Stoker's *Dracula* was published on May 26, 1897. Countless vampire books and stories have been written since. Tales about creatures who sip human blood, sleep in coffins, and live forever continue to thrill people. These tales generate lines at book stores and fill movie theaters. Everyone knows there is no such thing as a real vampire. Like thrill rides at an amusement park, these stories are terrifying, but safe.

1. What point does the author make in this selection? Do you agree? Why or why not?

   _____

   _____

2. What happened on May 26, 1897? _____

3. How many vampire books have been published? Is that a fact or an opinion? Is it possible to know the exact number? Why or why not?

   _____

   _____

4. What titles and statistics could the author have included to prove vampire films fill theaters?

   _____

   _____

5. Why does the author compare vampire stories to thrill rides at an amusement park? What kind of evidence could the author have included to support that statement?

   _____

   _____

CCSS.ELA-Literacy.RI.6.9: Compare and contrast one author's presentation of events with that of another (e.g., a memoir written by and a biography on the same person).

Directions: Read about the life of Helen Keller at the Helen Keller International website. <http://www.hki.org/about-helen-keller/helen-kellers-life/>
Then, read "Chapter 1" of *The Story of My Life* by Helen Keller at <http://digital.library.upenn.edu/women/keller/life/life.html>.

On another piece of paper, write a paragraph or two comparing the two works.

Name: _____ Date: _____

WRITING—SECTION THEME: WRITING OPINION PIECES

CCSS.ELA-Literacy.W.6.1: Write arguments to support claims with clear reasons and relevant evidence.

What I Think: Presenting an Opinion

CCSS.ELA-Literacy.W.6.1a: Introduce claim(s) and organize the reasons and evidence clearly.

Directions: Read the question. Write your opinion, a reason, and an example below.

Question: Should school vending machines sell soda?

1. Write a sentence stating your opinion. _____
   _____
   _____

2. Write a reason for your opinion. Be specific. _____
   _____
   _____
   _____

3. Supply evidence to support your reason. You might offer an example from your own experience.

   _____
   _____
   _____
   _____

CCSS.ELA-Literacy.W.6.1b: Support claim(s) with clear reasons and relevant evidence, using credible sources and demonstrating an understanding of the topic or text.

Directions: On another paper, write an essay starting with the answers you wrote above. Add two more reasons for a total of three. Then use the library or Internet to gather relevant information. Add statistics and quotations from experts to support your points.

Name: _____   Date: _____

WRITING OPINION PIECES – *Nevertheless* and Other Joiners

CCSS.ELA-Literacy.W.6.1c: Use words, phrases, and clauses to clarify the relationships among claim(s) and reasons.

Directions: Write a sentence stating your opinion about the following question.

     Question: Should all students be required to read the same book for class?

_____

_____

Then, in a paragraph, defend your position. Use appropriate words and phrases to connect each of your claims to its supporting reason. Examples include *because, since, yet, in spite of, regardless of, even so, however, nevertheless, granted that, as long as, unless, while, with this in mind,* and *due to*.

_____

_____

_____

_____

_____

_____

_____

_____

_____

_____

_____

Name: _____   Date: _____

WRITING OPINION PIECES – Dressed to Impress: Using Formal Language

CCSS.ELA-Literacy.W.6.1d: Establish and maintain a formal style.

Directions: Write a letter to the mayor. Ask that your town consider building a recreation center, skate park, water park, performance center, or other facility. Include at least two good reasons for your request. Use correct business letter form and formal language. To set the right tone, imagine that, dressed in your best clothes, you enter the mayor's office. An aide introduces you, and you shake hands. You sit in a leather chair across a broad polished desk from the mayor, who is wearing a business suit. Remember, your ideas are important and you want to convince him or her.

_____

_____

_____

_____

_____

_____

_____

_____

_____

_____

_____

_____

_____

Challenge: On another paper, write the same arguments as an email to a close friend. How are the two notes the same? How are they different? Why do the differences matter?

Name: _____ Date: _____

WRITING OPINION PIECES – Clinching the Deal: Writing a Conclusion

CCSS.ELA-Literacy.W.6.1e: Provide a concluding statement or section that follows from the argument presented.

Directions: A concluding statement helps the reader understand and remember the points you have made in a text. Read the following passage.

> Summer break gives students a chance to develop physically. It allows them to spend more time outdoors. Summer is a great time for students to explore individual creative interests. Even academic pursuits such as science, literature, and math can benefit from a summer break. Many individual students have special talents and interests. Often, they use unstructured time to explore more advanced material.

1. Write a closing statement that sums up the author's point of view.

    _____

    _____

2. Write a paragraph supporting the opposite position. The opening statement is provided. Don't forget to supply a conclusion. You probably don't agree with this opinion, but that doesn't matter. This is an exercise in writing and thinking. Reasons often offered for this view include: boredom, mischief, lack of supervision, forgetting learned facts and skills, parent childcare issues, and unused school buildings.

    During summer break, students lose valuable learning time. _____

    _____

    _____

    _____

    _____

    _____

Challenge: Putting it all Together

Use resources such as the library and the Internet to gather information about the advantages and disadvantages of a summer break. Form an opinion based on the data you find. On your own paper, write a short essay stating your opinion, offering informed reasons for it, and closing with a convincing summary of your ideas.

Name: _____ Date: _____

WRITING—SECTION THEME: WRITING INFORMATIVE AND EXPLANATORY TEXTS

CCSS.ELA-Literacy.W.6.2: Write informative/explanatory texts to examine a topic and convey ideas, concepts, and information through the selection, organization, and analysis of relevant content.

Making Ideas Clear: Using Text Structure to Organize an Essay

CCSS.ELA-Literacy.W.6.2a: Introduce a topic; organize ideas, concepts, and information, using strategies such as definition, classification, comparison/contrast, and cause/effect; include formatting (e.g., headings), graphics (e.g., charts, tables), and multimedia when useful to aiding comprehension.

Directions: On this page, write a short essay comparing your elementary school to your middle school. Include headings and graphic elements such as hand-drawn maps, graphs, or charts.

_____
_____
_____
_____
_____
_____
_____
_____
_____
_____

The text you have just written uses comparison and contrast as an organizational structure. Other possible structures include sequence, description, definition, classification, and cause/effect.

Directions: Using middle school as the topic, write another short essay on your own paper using a different structure. For example, you might write a definition of middle school (definition), types of students you have met (classification), what happens if you forget to do your homework (cause and effect), or making friends in middle school (problem and solution). Don't forget to use headings and graphic elements such as maps, sketches, or charts.

Name: _____   Date: _____

WRITING INFORMATIVE AND EXPLANATORY TEXTS –
Filling in the Blanks: Adding Details and Examples

CCSS.ELA-Literacy.W.6.2b: Develop the topic with relevant facts, definitions, concrete details, quotations, or other information and examples.

Directions: Write a short essay explaining your favorite team or sport or your favorite game. Imagine your reader has never heard of your subject. You will need to define special terms, discuss details such as team size and equipment, and explain the object of the game. If you have a favorite quotation from a famous coach or player, include it.

_____

_____

_____

_____

_____

_____

_____

_____

_____

_____

_____

_____

_____

_____

_____

_____

_____

_____

Name: _____ Date: _____

WRITING INFORMATIVE AND EXPLANATORY TEXTS –
Connecting Ideas: Using Transitions

CCSS.ELA-Literacy.W.6.2c: Use appropriate transitions to clarify the relationships among ideas and concepts.

When ideas are not connected, it is hard for readers to follow what the writer is trying to say. That's why transitional words, phrases, sentences, and passages are important.

Directions: Write a transitional sentence to connect the ideas in each pair of sentences below. Use words and phrases such as *for example, however, while this may be true, consequently, after, meanwhile, subsequently, nearby, around, even though, similarly, certainly, especially, since, because,* and *therefore.*

1. On June 1, Amelia Earhart took off, hoping to set a world record by flying around the world at the equator.

   _____

   _____

   Ships and planes searched for the wreckage of her plane for weeks, but it was never found.

2. Henry Ford developed an efficient way to manufacture his Model T, making it affordable.

   _____

   _____

   _____

   Soon, horses, buggies, and wagons started to disappear from city streets.

3. Abraham Lincoln was sworn in as President of the United States on March 4, 1861.

   _____

   _____

   In the spring of 1865, Lincoln's funeral train, draped in black bunting, snaked slowly through the countryside.

4. On your own paper, write a short paragraph explaining what you did yesterday. Start with a sentence about the morning. End with a sentence about the evening and include one or two transitional sentences.

Name: _____ Date: _____

WRITING INFORMATIVE AND EXPLANATORY TEXTS –
Special Words for Special Topics

CCSS.ELA-Literacy.W.6.2d: Use precise language and domain-specific vocabulary to inform about or explain the topic.

Using the right words for your subject can save time and confusion. For example, in geography, there are no good alternatives for terms such as *equator, latitude, longitude,* and *compass rose*. People also use special terms when talking about their interests and activities.

Directions: Write a short essay explaining a hobby or activity you know well. It could be model railroading, singing, acting, dancing, rock climbing, playing a musical instrument, carpentry, cooking, art, photography, reading, or video gaming. Use precise vocabulary to describe the equipment you use and the skills you have acquired. After you finish the piece, circle each special term.

_____

_____

_____

_____

_____

_____

_____

_____

_____

_____

_____

_____

_____

_____

_____

_____

_____

Name: _____   Date: _____

WRITING INFORMATIVE AND EXPLANATORY TEXTS – Fitting the Occasion

CCSS.ELA-Literacy.W.6.2e: Establish and maintain a formal style.

Writers of reports and informative essays usually use a formal style. They include precise vocabulary and avoid colloquial phrases such as *a whole lot of.*

Directions: Read each informal sentence below. Rewrite it in a formal style.

1. Anyways, more than two hundred thousand people got together on August 28, 1963, for this thing called the "March on Washington."

   _____

   _____

2. There are whole bunches of different ways to make a graph.

   _____

   _____

3. Natural camouflage is all about keeping critters from getting eaten.

   _____

   _____

4. Back in the day, peeps didn't know how diseases got around.

   _____

   _____

5. Sound waves go pretty fast, but yet light waves go even quicker.

   _____

   _____

6. Scientists know lots of stuff about volcanoes.

   _____

   _____

   _____

7. And while I'm at it, I may as well tell you about Jane Goodall's work with chimps.

   _____

   _____

WRITING INFORMATIVE AND EXPLANATORY TEXTS –
Sum it Up Beautifully

CCSS.ELA-Literacy.W.6.2f: Provide a concluding statement or section that follows from the information or explanation presented.

Directions: Read the selection below and answer the questions that follow.

Scientists had been trying to transmit moving images since the late 1800s. In fact, the word television was coined in 1900. Many early advances were made in Europe. At the same time, Americans were working on an electronic system, and at first, it was plagued by problems. By the end of the 1920s, developers had finally made it work. In 1928, there were a few broadcasts in the United States. They did not have many viewers. Most people still listened to shows on the radio. Network television did not appear until the late 1940s. In the boom times after World War II, families had more money. They were able to buy television sets.

1. What is the main idea of this selection?

   _____

   _____

   _____

2. Is this text structured using cause and effect, comparison and contrast, sequence, problem and solution, or description?

   _____

3. Consider the structure and content of the passage. Then write a concluding sentence.

   _____

   _____

   _____

Challenge: Use the Internet or the library to find out about early television shows. On your own paper, write a short essay reporting your discoveries. Close with a sentence or paragraph that sums up the most important ideas.

Name: _____ Date: _____

WRITING—SECTION THEME: WRITING NARRATIVES

CCSS.ELA-Literacy.W.6.3: Write narratives to develop real or imagined experiences or events using effective technique, relevant descriptive details, and well-structured event sequences.

The Story Machine

CCSS.ELA-Literacy.W.6.3a: Engage and orient the reader by establishing a context and introducing a narrator and/or characters; organize an event sequence that unfolds naturally and logically.

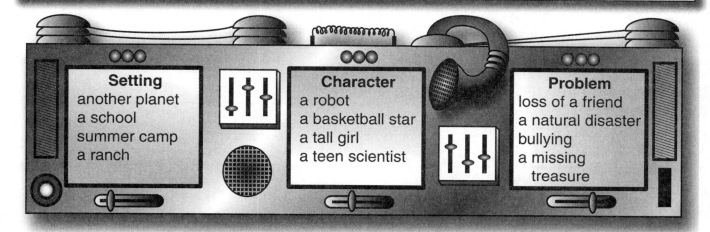

Setting	Character	Problem
another planet	a robot	loss of a friend
a school	a basketball star	a natural disaster
summer camp	a tall girl	bullying
a ranch	a teen scientist	a missing treasure

Directions: Choose any setting, any character, and any problem from the story machine. Combine them to create a short story. You can add other characters. You can also add other elements, such as time and weather, to the setting. Each event in the story should lead to the next. Continue the story on your own paper, if you need more space.

_____

_____

_____

_____

_____

_____

_____

_____

_____

_____

_____

Name: _____ Date: _____

WRITING NARRATIVES – Observe!

CCSS.ELA-Literacy.W.6.3b: Use narrative techniques, such as dialogue, pacing, and description, to develop experiences, events, and/or characters.

Directions: Read the directions below. Complete each part of the exercise before moving to the next.

1. Write a short paragraph describing your favorite food. Include how it looks, how it smells, and how it feels in your mouth (crunchy, silky, smooth, crisp), as well as how it tastes.

_____

_____

_____

_____

_____

_____

2. Write a short discussion between two characters involving the food you just described. One loves the dish, but the other hates it because it brings back bad memories.

_____

_____

_____

_____

_____

_____

3. Use the description and the dialogue you have just written as part of an original short story. The two passages do not have to be at the beginning. They don't even have to be together. They just have to appear somewhere in the story. Write the story on your own paper.

    As you begin to write, consider the following:
    • Which of these two characters is the narrator?
    • What problem does the narrator have?
    • What will happen if the problem is not solved?
    • What is the time frame?

Name: _____   Date: _____

WRITING NARRATIVES – Moving Right Along

CCSS.ELA-Literacy.W.6.3c: Use a variety of transition words, phrases, and clauses to convey sequence and signal shifts from one time frame or setting to another.

Directions: In a narrative, transition words make changes in time or place clearer to readers. Circle the time transition word or phrase under each sentence that fits best in each blank.

1. The old horse was plodding along the familiar trail. _____ the ground began to shake.

    Formerly   Suddenly   Whenever

2. Amanda whipped around _____ she heard Lacey scream.

    to begin with   in the first place   as soon as

3. Mike reached the top of the hill _____ to see smoke rising in the distance.

    just in time   in the meantime   in due time

Directions: Write a sentence using each location transition word or phrase.

4. adjacent to _____

    _____

5. opposite _____

    _____

6. beneath _____

    _____

Challenge: On your own paper, tell the story of a lost pet from the animal's point of view. Use time and place transition words.

Name: _____   Date: _____

WRITING NARRATIVES – Make it Vivid

CCSS.ELA-Literacy.W.6.3d: Use precise words and phrases, relevant descriptive details, and sensory language to convey experiences and events.

Stories become exciting when readers can see, hear, and feel what is going on. Writers use sensory words and details to create the illusion of reality.

Directions: Read the directions below. Complete each part of the exercise before moving to the next.

1. Imagine a place you remember well. It can be comfortable, frightening, exciting, or dull. It can be your room at home, your route to school, or even the room where you are sitting now. Remember or notice as many details about the scene as you can. Include smells, textures, temperatures, and sounds as well as things you see. Use those details to write a description. When you finish, circle each sensory detail.

   _____

   _____

   _____

   _____

   _____

   _____

   _____

2. Imagine an animal you have seen often. Use sensory words and details to describe the way it looks, sounds, smells, and feels. Think about its eyes, nose, mouth, teeth, fur, skin, tail, legs, and paws/feet. Is it scrawny or chubby? How does it move? Consider the emotional connotations of the words you choose.

   _____

   _____

   _____

   _____

   _____

3. On your own paper, combine the place you described and the animal you described to create an original story. When your narrator finds or meets the animal in that place, there is some kind of urgent problem the narrator must solve.

Name: _____ Date: _____

WRITING NARRATIVES – So What Happened?

CCSS.ELA-Literacy.W.6.3e: Provide a conclusion that follows from the narrated experiences or events.

Most stories have a problem that is resolved near the end. Sometimes main characters get what they want, and other times they don't. When you tell friends about a frightening experience, they always want to know what happened. What they are requesting is your story's conclusion.

Directions: Write a possible conclusion for each set of story events. This should just be a short sentence that sums up what happens.

1. There is a boating accident.   Two friends swim to a small island.

   _____

2. A family is hiking.   A rock slide blocks the return path.

   _____

3. Shawn's friend Jason cheats.   Shawn tries to help.

   _____

4. Britta's ring is stolen.   Britta tries to find out who took it.

   _____

5. Mike thinks his dad is dead.   His dad returns.

   _____

CCSS.ELA-Literacy.W.6.4: Produce clear and coherent writing in which the development, organization, and style are appropriate to task, purpose, and audience.

Directions: On your own paper, write a story using one of the five possible plots outlined above. Create a narrator and develop other characters. Use sensory details and precise vocabulary to make the setting real. Include time and place transition words.

Name: _____ Date: _____

WRITING NARRATIVES – Building a Critique Group

CCSS.ELA-Literacy.W.6.5: With some guidance and support from peers and adults, develop and strengthen writing as needed by planning, revising, editing, rewriting, or trying a new approach.

Because authors often have trouble spotting problems in their own work, many share manuscripts with small groups of fellow writers. These peers point out the best things about a story or article. Then they make suggestions for improvement.

Directions: You are going to share your best story or article with a critique group. Write five rules you think the members should follow.

1. _____

2. _____

3. _____

4. _____

5. _____

Find out which rules others listed most often. Use those rules to create a set of critique guidelines. After the critique session, discuss the process. Reevaluate the guidelines if necessary.

Writing for a Class Magazine

CCSS.ELA-Literacy.W.6.6: Use technology, including the Internet, to produce and publish writing as well as to interact and collaborate with others.
CCSS.ELA-Literacy.W.6.7: Conduct short research projects to answer a question, drawing on several sources and refocusing the inquiry when appropriate.
CCSS.ELA-Literacy.W.6.8: Gather relevant information from multiple print and digital sources; assess the credibility of each source; and quote or paraphrase the data and conclusions of others while avoiding plagiarism and providing basic bibliographic information for sources.

Directions: Use several sources to find the answer to an interesting question. It could be related to a class trip, a speaker, or a unit of study. On your own paper, write a short article based on your information. Include a bibliography listing the books, magazine articles, and websites you consulted. After revising the article with the help of your critique group, use a word processor to prepare it for publication. Include it in a printed or digital class magazine.

Name: _____   Date: _____

WRITING—SECTION THEME: DRAWING EVIDENCE FROM TEXT

CCSS.ELA-Literacy.W.6.9: Draw evidence from literary or informational texts to support analysis, reflection, and research.

Compare Genres

CCSS.ELA-Literacy.W.6.9a: Apply Grade 6 Reading Standards to literature (e.g., "Compare and contrast texts in different forms or genres [e.g., stories and poems; historical novels and fantasy stories] in terms of their approaches to similar themes and topics").

Directions: Read "The Last Leaf" by O. Henry (William Sydney Porter) and "One Art" by Elizabeth Bishop. They can be found online at: <http://www.classicshorts.com/stories/lastleaf.html> and <http://www.poetryfoundation.org/poem/176996>. Answer the questions below.

1. Name three ways the two works are different. Be specific. _____

    _____

    _____

2. In both "The Last Leaf" and "One Art," certain things are lost. What is lost in each work?

    _____

    _____

3. How is repetition used in each work? _____

    _____

4. In each work, a person says something he or she does not mean. Who is that person in "The Last Leaf"? How do you know? In the last stanza of "One Art," what does the speaker really mean?

    _____

    _____

    _____

CCSS.ELA-Literacy.W.6.9b: Apply Grade 6 Reading Standards to literary nonfiction. (**CCSS.ELA-Literacy.RI.6.6:** Determine an author's point of view or purpose in a text and explain how it is conveyed in the text.)

Directions: Read Chapter 1 of *Narrative of the Life of Frederick Douglass an American Slave Written by Himself* by Frederick Douglass <http://www.gutenberg.org/files/23/23-h/23-h.htm>. On another paper, write a short essay exploring the author's point of view and how it is expressed in this chapter.

Name: _____ Date: _____

SPEAKING AND LISTENING—SECTION THEME: DISCUSSIONS

CCSS.ELA-Literacy.SL.6.1: Engage effectively in a range of collaborative discussions (one-on-one, in groups, and teacher-led) with diverse partners on grade 6 topics, texts, and issues, building on others' ideas and expressing their own clearly.

Be Prepared

CCSS.ELA-Literacy.SL.6.1a: Come to discussions prepared, having read or studied required material; explicitly draw on that preparation by referring to evidence on the topic, text, or issue to probe and reflect on ideas under discussion.

Directions: Answer the questions below.

1. What happens if you or others in your group do not read or study the material before a discussion?

   _____

   _____

   _____

2. How can you remember information to share in a discussion?

   _____

   _____

   _____

3. What happens if everyone makes generalizations in a discussion without including evidence from reading or study?

   _____

   _____

   _____

Challenge: Prepare to enjoy a class discussion about the future of artificial intelligence and robotics. Read "Robots and AI" by Matt, a former Athena Student Intern at <http://robotics.nasa.gov/students/ai_robotics.php>. Follow the included links to find out more about robots and artificial intelligence. Jot down information and questions to share on your own paper.

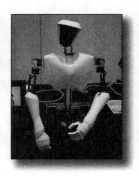

Name: _____ Date: _____

DISCUSSIONS – Sharing Ideas

CCSS.ELA-Literacy.SL.6.1b: Follow rules for collegial discussions, set specific goals and deadlines, and define individual roles as needed.

Directions: List four rules participants should follow in a discussion.

1. _____

_____

2. _____

_____

3. _____

_____

4. _____

_____

CCSS.ELA-Literacy.SL.6.1c: Pose and respond to specific questions with elaboration and detail by making comments that contribute to the topic, text, or issue under discussion.

Directions: Write three questions you could ask in a discussion about a civics, science, or literature topic you have covered recently in class.

1. _____

_____

2. _____

_____

3. _____

_____

During the course of a discussion, ask one of your questions. In addition, offer an answer to another participant's question or add information to another participant's comment.

Name: _____　　Date: _____

DISCUSSIONS – Discussion Reflections

CCSS.ELA-Literacy.SL.6.1d: Review the key ideas expressed and demonstrate understanding of multiple perspectives through reflection and paraphrasing.

Directions: On the chart below, jot down one important idea expressed in a group discussion.

Idea

_____

_____

_____

Paraphrase (Write the idea in your own words.)

_____

_____

_____

Another View (Write another participant's opinion about the same subject.)

_____

_____

_____

Another View or Additional Information (if applicable)

_____

_____

_____

Alternate activity: If you do not have access to a discussion group, view a TED talk for kids at <http://www.ted.com/playlists/86/for_kids> or an online documentary film such as those listed at <http://www.watchknowlearn.org/Category.aspx?CategoryID=14808>. Use the chart above to record and reflect on one of the ideas presented.

Name: _____   Date: _____

SPEAKING AND LISTENING—SECTION THEME: DIVERSE MEDIA AND FORMATS

CCSS.ELA-Literacy.SL.6.2: Interpret information presented in diverse media and formats (e.g., visually, quantitatively, orally) and explain how it contributes to a topic, text, or issue under study.

Experiencing a Great Speech

CCSS.ELA-Literacy.SL.6.3: Delineate a speaker's argument and specific claims, distinguishing claims that are supported by reasons and evidence from claims that are not.

Directions: Follow the link below. Read a short introduction to Lincoln's Gettysburg Address. Study the picture on the page and then listen to W.F. Hooley deliver the speech. <http://publicdomainreview.org/collections/w-f-hooley-reads-lincolns-gettysburg-address-1898/>

1. What does the picture add to your understanding of the speech? What does the written text contribute? What did the audio presentation add? Was the introduction helpful? Why or why not?

   _____

   _____

   _____

   _____

2. What argument does President Lincoln make in this speech? What specific claims does he make? What evidence does he offer for them?

   _____

   _____

   _____

   _____

3. How do you think your experience of this speech differs from the experience of those who heard it in person?

   _____

   _____

   _____

Name: _____ Date: _____

DIVERSE MEDIA AND FORMATS – Delivering a Talk

CCSS.ELA-Literacy.SL.6.4: Present claims and findings, sequencing ideas logically and using pertinent descriptions, facts, and details to accentuate main ideas or themes; use appropriate eye contact, adequate volume, and clear pronunciation.

Directions: Plan a short talk about an inventor.

1. What did the person invent or discover? _____

_____

2. When did the person live and how did their invention or discovery change life for other people at the time? Include descriptions and statistics.

_____

_____

_____

3. How did the invention or discovery change the inventor's life? _____

_____

_____

4. Why did you find this particular person interesting, inspiring, or important?

_____

_____

5. In conclusion, what do you want listeners to remember about this person?

_____

_____

CCSS.ELA-Literacy.SL.6.5: Include multimedia components (e.g., graphics, images, music, sound) and visual displays in presentations to clarify information.
CCSS.ELA-Literacy.SL.6.6: Adapt speech to a variety of contexts and tasks, demonstrating command of formal English when indicated or appropriate. (See Grade 6 Language Standards 1 and 3 here for specific expectations.)

Directions: Deliver your talk to a group, or if this is not possible, record your speech so you can play it back. Use note cards to keep track of your main points. Rehearse your speech several times before you deliver it. Speak slowly and clearly. Look at the audience or camera as much as possible. Use digital slides, transparencies, or posters to help listeners visualize the inventor, the invention, and the workshop or lab. Include music or sound effects, if appropriate.

Name: _____ Date: _____

LANGUAGE—SECTION THEME: STANDARD ENGLISH AND GRAMMAR USAGE

CCSS.ELA-Literacy.L.6.1: Demonstrate command of the conventions of standard English grammar and usage when writing or speaking.

Three Cases for Pronouns

CCSS.ELA-Literacy.L.6.1a: Ensure that pronouns are in the proper case (subjective, objective, possessive).

Directions: Pronouns have subjective, objective, and possessive forms. Circle the correct forms in each sentence.

1. Because Gregor Mendel was curious, (him, he, his) wondered how pea plants passed traits down to (they, them, their) offspring, and so he designed experiments to study (they, them, their).

2. In a famous Greek myth, Venus feels sorry for a sculptor (who, whom, whose) has fallen in love with (he, his, him) statue, so (she, her, herself) transforms the sculpture into a real woman.

3. The bus driver ordered Rosa Parks to surrender (she, her) seat to a white man, but (she, her, herself) refused to obey (he, him, his).

4. When (we, us, our) study geography, we use (we, us, our) textbooks as well as the Internet and other resources available to (we, us, our).

5. (You, Your, Yourself) are certain to find information about (you, your, yourself) favorite animal online.

6. (I, Me, My) know (you, your) have (I, me, my) book because (I, me, my) gave (it, its) to (you, your) when (you, your) asked (I, me, my) to borrow (it, its).

Challenge: List the pronouns that are used as subjects in the sentences above. On your own paper, write a paragraph using all of them.

_____

_____

Name: _____ Date: _____

STANDARD ENGLISH AND GRAMMAR USAGE –
That's Intense

CCSS.ELA-Literacy.L.6.1b: Use intensive pronouns (e.g., myself, ourselves).

Intensive pronouns add emphasis to a pronoun. For example, consider the two sentences, "I will do it myself." and "I will do it." How do their meanings differ?

Directions: Circle the intensive pronouns that belong in the sentences below.

1. If the boys complete that project by (theirselves, theirself, themselves), Principal Hayes (himself, hisself, hisselves) will congratulate them.

2. You two girls must care for that dog (yourself, yourselves, youself), because I (myself, myselves, mineself) am unwilling to assume your responsibilities.

3. We are planning to bring all the food (ourselves, ourself, ourselfs), but guests should clean up after (theyself, themselves, theyselves).

4. That report is not going to write (itself, itsself, isselve), so you (yerselve, youself, yourself) should start working on it.

Challenge: Write a short paragraph using at least four intensive pronouns.

_____

_____

_____

_____

_____

_____

_____

_____

_____

Name: _____   Date: _____

STANDARD ENGLISH AND GRAMMAR USAGE –
Do Your Pronouns Agree?

CCSS.ELA-Literacy.L.6.1c: Recognize and correct inappropriate shifts in pronoun number and person.*

Pronouns should agree with the nouns they refer to in number and person.

Directions: Underline the correct ending for each sentence. Then answer the question.

1. When Brittany arrived at school,

   a. they were supposed to take their seats and start work right away.

   b. she was supposed to take her seat and start work right away.

   Which two pronouns agree with Brittany? _____ _____

2. We bring umbrellas because

   a. we always need them in the afternoon.

   b. you always need one in the afternoon.

   Who needs umbrellas? _____

   Which pronoun agrees with umbrellas? _____

3. Jason just found out that

   a. he should sign up early for band.

   b. you should sign up early for band.

   Which pronoun agrees with Jason? _____

4. When Jake went to the park,

   a. he was supposed to meet his teacher by the lake.

   b. they were supposed to meet their teacher by the lake.

   Which pronouns agree with Jake? _____ _____

Name: _____ Date: _____

STANDARD ENGLISH AND GRAMMAR USAGE –
Fixing Vague Pronouns

CCSS.ELA-Literacy.L.6.1d: Recognize and correct vague pronouns (i.e., ones with unclear or ambiguous antecedents).*

Readers should not have to wonder which noun a pronoun refers to.

Directions: Circle the vague pronoun in each sentence. Rewrite the sentence to make it clear.

1. When Carly and Maria arrived at the party, she hurried into the kitchen to put the drinks in the refrigerator.

   _____

   _____

2. The school rules prohibited wearing t-shirts with logos, which many students resented.

   _____

   _____

3. As soon as Jason and Michael told their parents about the tournament, they started making plans.

   _____

   _____

4. Before Shawn started studying piano with Mr. DeLawrence, he had performed on concert stages around the world.

   _____

   _____

5. Sam called Carlos soon after he was hired.

   _____

   _____

6. Claudia bought her sister a tablet computer, which she took with her to college.

   _____

   _____

Name: _____ Date: _____

STANDARD ENGLISH AND GRAMMAR USAGE –
Botched Pronouns

CCSS.ELA-Literacy.L.6.1e: Recognize variations from standard English in their own and others' writing and speaking, and identify and use strategies to improve expression in conventional language.*

Directions: Rewrite each sentence using standard English, and explain why each sentence was incorrect.

1. That lunch is for her and I.

    _____

    Why was the sentence incorrect?

    _____

    _____

2. Myself and her will accept the award tonight.

    _____

    Why was the sentence incorrect?

    _____

    _____

3. Remember, this is between you and I.

    _____

    Why was the sentence incorrect?

    _____

    _____

4. Whomever can hit the ball over the fence, is a better batter than I.

    _____

    Why was the sentence incorrect?

    _____

    _____

Name: _____ Date: _____

LANGUAGE—SECTION THEME: CAPITALIZATION, PUNCTUATION, AND SPELLING

CCSS.ELA-Literacy.L.6.2: Demonstrate command of the conventions of standard English capitalization, punctuation, and spelling when writing.

Extra! Extra!

CCSS.ELA-Literacy.L.6.2a: Use punctuation (commas, parentheses, dashes) to set off non-restrictive/parenthetical elements.*

A nonrestrictive clause contains information about a person, place, or thing that could be removed from the sentence without changing the meaning of the sentence. A nonrestrictive clause is set off from the rest of the sentence with commas. Parentheses and dashes are other punctuation marks used to set off elements that are not essential to the meaning of a sentence.

Directions: Add a set of commas to set off the nonrestrictive clause in the following sentences.

1. West Hills Courthouse which has been protected by legislation for over a decade could be demolished soon.

2. This winter the coldest in recent memory is almost over.

Directions: Add parentheses to set off nonessential elements in the following sentences.

3. The constellation Cassiopeia named after an ancient queen of Ethiopia is often easy to spot in the night sky.

4. This week's book fair will 1 raise money for the school library, 2 enable readers to meet their favorite authors, and 3 encourage more students to read for entertainment.

Directions: Add a set of dashes to set off parenthetical elements in the following sentences.

5. My sister the best in the whole world has invited me to join her on a backpacking trip this summer.

6. Our new coach the great Steve Allard will meet us at the park on Saturday morning.

Directions: Write a sentence using commas, parentheses, or dashes to set off a parenthetical phrase.

7. _____

    _____

    _____

Name: _____ Date: _____

CAPITALIZATION, PUNCTUATION, AND SPELLING – Spell it Right!

CCSS.ELA-Literacy.L.6.2b: Spell correctly.

Directions: Complete the following exercises about spelling.

1. Explain why correct spelling is important.

    _____

    _____

    _____

2. Name two resources that can help you locate the correct spelling of a word.

    a. _____

    b. _____

3. How can critique groups help writers detect spelling errors?

    _____

    _____

    _____

4. Circle the three incorrectly spelled words.

    exhibit   disgize   detane   smudge   through

    barbecue   partial   expecially   sophomore

5. Write the correct spellings of those words.

    _____   _____   _____

Challenge: Edit the draft of another student's essay. Use a colored pen to write a small *sp* (short for *spelling error*) beside each misspelled word.

Name: _____ Date: _____

LANGUAGE—SECTION THEME: USING LANGUAGE

CCSS.ELA-Literacy.L.6.3: Use knowledge of language and its conventions when writing, speaking, reading, or listening.

Creating Sentence Variety

CCSS.ELA-Literacy.L.6.3a: Vary sentence patterns for meaning, reader/listener interest, and style.*

Directions: Change the order of clauses to write two additional versions of each sentence.

Example:

   a. El Greco painted *View of Toledo* at a time when few other Spanish artists tackled landscapes.

   b. At a time when few other Spanish artists tackled landscapes, El Greco painted *A View of Toledo*.

   c. Few other Spanish artists tackled landscapes at the time when El Greco painted *A View of Toledo*.

1. a. The Montgolfier brothers designed a hot-air balloon that carried two pilots aloft in Paris on November 21, 1783.

   b. _____

     _____

   c. _____

     _____

2. a. Sir Edmund Hillary and Tenzing Norgay became the first climbers to reach the summit of Mt. Everest on May 29, 1953.

   b. _____

     _____

   c. _____

     _____

Challenge: On your own paper, write a paragraph about a favorite book, song, movie, or television show. Use short and long sentences, questions, and structural variation to hold the interest of your readers.

Name: _____ Date: _____

USING LANGUAGE – Formal and Informal Styles

CCSS.ELA-Literacy.L.6.3b: Maintain consistency in style and tone.*

Directions: Circle the words or phrases that do not fit in the following passage. Then rewrite the paragraph as directed.

> The spleen filters blood, removing old blood cells from circulation. This organ, which weighs about five ounces, does other cool stuff such as like recycling iron and creating antibodies to fight invading bacteria. While this stuff is important, it's not vital. Some people have their spleens removed due to an illness or injury. The surgery has some effects, but they are not life-threatening.

Rewrite the passage using a formal style throughout. (Imagine this is part of a report for your biology class.)

_____

_____

_____

_____

_____

_____

_____

Rewrite the passage using an informal style throughout. (Imagine you are explaining your dad's surgery to a friend in an email.)

_____

_____

_____

_____

_____

_____

_____

Name: _____ Date: _____

USING LANGUAGE – What Does it Mean?: Deciphering Unfamiliar Words

CCSS.ELA-Literacy.L.6.4: Determine or clarify the meaning of unknown and multiple-meaning words and phrases based on grade 6 reading and content, choosing flexibly from a range of strategies.

Directions: Complete the following exercises on word meaning.

1. When you encounter an unfamiliar word in a text, how can you determine its meaning? Name three possible approaches.

   a. _____

   b. _____

   c. _____

2. Write the meaning of each underlined word.

   a. The <u>arboreal</u> monkeys spent very little time on the ground, preferring the leafy rain forest canopy.

   _____

   _____

   b. Invasive tamarisks were starting to <u>encroach</u> on the riverbanks, pushing out native shrubs and trees.

   _____

   c. The new student managed to <u>amass</u> an amazing amount of support for his candidacy.

   _____

   d. Daniel was <u>mortified</u> when he discovered that everyone knew about his failure.

   _____

   e. A shocking web of <u>intrigue</u> surrounded the assassination of Abraham Lincoln.

   _____

   f. Every subject and field of interest develops its own private set of words, or <u>jargon</u>.

   _____

   g. During World War II, Great Britain found itself in a <u>perilous</u> position.

   _____

Name: _____   Date: _____

USING LANGUAGE – Using Context

CCSS.ELA-Literacy.L.6.4a: Use context (e.g., the overall meaning of a sentence or paragraph; a word's position or function in a sentence) as a clue to the meaning of a word or phrase.

Directions: Circle the meaning of each underlined word. Use context clues.

1. People often visit the desert for its <u>solitude</u>, but they are seldom alone, since this unique landscape hosts an impressive variety of plant and animal life.

   a. warmth   b. dryness   c. privacy   d. none of these

2. According to Longfellow's famous poem, Paul Revere spread the <u>alarm</u>, telling the Minutemen that the Redcoats were on their way.

   a. warning   b. panic   c. siren   d. none of these

3. Visitors to the Amazon rain forest should prepare for <u>copious</u> amounts of precipitation.

   a. plentiful   b. slight   c. moderate   d. none of these

4. The <u>luminous</u> veil you sometimes see stretched across the night sky is actually blended light from billions of distant stars in our galaxy, the Milky Way.

   a. thick   b. thin   c. glowing   d. none of these

5. During the Cold War, peace groups <u>denounced</u> policies that led to rapidly growing stockpiles of nuclear weapons in both Russia and the United States.

   a. advocated   b. condemned   c. published   d. none of these

6. Because citizens hold differing opinions and vote for different candidates, presidential elections are never <u>unanimous</u>.

   a. undivided   b. unusual   c. disputed   d. none of these

7. Even when the number of jobs grew during World War II, the <u>chronic</u> problem of employment discrimination against blacks did not improve.

   a. slight   b. constant   c. brief   d. none of these

8. Though nobody can see it, the <u>equator</u> passes through several nations on the continent of South America.

   a. an imaginary line   b. a kind of bear   c. a king   d. none of these

Name: _____ Date: _____

USING LANGUAGE – Using Greek and Latin Affixes and Roots to Build Vocabulary

CCSS.ELA-Literacy.L.6.4b: Use common, grade-appropriate Greek or Latin affixes and roots as clues to the meaning of a word (e.g., audience, auditory, audible).

Directions: Answer the following questions about word meanings.

1. If *audio* means "sound," which of the five human senses does an *audiologist* study?

   _____

2. If *equi-* means "the same or even" and *lateral* means "side," what can you say about an *equilateral* triangle?

   _____

3. If *circum-* means "around" and *navi* means "to sail," what feat do people who *circumnavigate* the globe accomplish?

   _____

4. If *sub-* means "below," *co-* means "with," and *ord* means "order," what's the difference between *to coordinate* and *to subordinate*?

   _____

   _____

5. If *muta* means "change," what does *mutation* mean?

   _____

6. If *sym-* means "together or with" and *bio-* means "life," what does *symbiosis* mean?

   _____

7. If *baro-* means "weight or pressure," and *meter* means "to measure," what characteristic of the atmosphere does a *barometer* measure?

   _____

8. If *-morph* means "form" and *a-* means "without," what does *amorphous* mean?

   _____

9. If *hydr-* means "water" and *de-* means "to remove," what is *dehydrated* food?

   _____

Challenge: On your own paper, write at least one other word that contains the same root as each of the underlined examples.

Name: _____ Date: _____

USING LANGUAGE – Check it Out: Using the Dictionary

CCSS.ELA-Literacy.L.6.4c: Consult reference materials (e.g., dictionaries, glossaries, thesauruses), both print and digital, to find the pronunciation of a word or determine or clarify its precise meaning or its part of speech.
CCSS.ELA-Literacy.L.6.4d: Verify the preliminary determination of the meaning of a word or phrase (e.g., by checking the inferred meaning in context or in a dictionary).

Directions: Use reference materials to answer each question.

1. Name two differences between the verb *to convict* and the noun *convict*.

   _____

   _____

   _____

2. Name two differences between the verb *to object* and the noun *object*.

   _____

   _____

   _____

3. Name two differences between the verb *to compact* and the noun *compact*.

   _____

   _____

   _____

4. Name two differences between the adjective *content* and the noun *content*.

   _____

   _____

   _____

5. Name two differences between the adjective *minute* and the noun *minute*.

   _____

   _____

   _____

Name: _____ Date: _____

LANGUAGE—SECTION THEME: FIGURATIVE LANGUAGE

CCSS.ELA-Literacy.L.6.5: Demonstrate understanding of figurative language, word relationships, and nuances in word meanings.

It's a Figure of Speech: Personification

CCSS.ELA-Literacy.L.6.5a: Interpret figures of speech (e.g., personification) in context.

Directions: Read each sentence and answer the questions that follow.

1. An irascible north wind, cloaked in ice, chased the last lovely day of autumn straight out of town.
   a. What is really happening in this sentence? _____
   _____
   b. What is the north wind compared to? _____
   c. What adjective is used to describe the wind's mood? _____
   d. What is the wind wearing? _____
   e. What did the wind do? _____

2. The computer stubbornly refused to start, complaining bitterly about a piece of new hardware that disagreed with its works.
   a. What is really happening in this sentence? _____
   _____
   b. What word describes the computer's attitude? _____
   c. Can a computer have an attitude? _____
   d. How do you think the computer really "complained"? _____
   _____
   e. What is the computer being compared to? _____

3. The figure of speech used in the sentences above is called **personification**. Write a sentence using personification to describe a rain or snow storm. Use verbs, adjectives, and adverbs that would usually apply to a person. How is the storm feeling? Because the storm is feeling this way, what human-like action does it perform? Does it throw things? Sweep things? Scream? Bellow?

   _____
   _____
   _____

Name: _____   Date: _____

FIGURATIVE LANGUAGE – Words That Belong Together

CCSS.ELA-Literacy.L.6.5b: Use the relationship between particular words (e.g., cause/effect, part/whole, item/category) to better understand each of the words.

Directions: Read each sentence and answer the questions that follow.

1. Heavy winter rains carry mud down into a canyon after an autumn fire denudes the slopes.
   a. Was the fire the cause or the effect of the mudslide? _____
   b. How does the meaning of the word *effect* help you understand the meaning of the word *cause*? _____
   _____

2. Every cell has a nucleus, cytoplasm, and a cell membrane.
   a. Is the nucleus part of the cell or the whole cell? _____
   b. How does the meaning of the word *part* help you understand the meaning of the word *whole*? _____
   _____

3. Planets in our solar system include Venus, Mercury, Earth, Mars, Jupiter, Saturn, Uranus, and Neptune.
   a. If Venus, Mercury, Earth, Mars, Jupiter, Uranus, and Neptune are items in a category, what is the category? _____
   b. How does the meaning of the word *items* help you understand the meaning of the word *category*? _____
   _____

4. The four inner planets are terrestrial, as opposed to the outer four, which are gas giants.
   a. How do the four inner planets compare with one another? _____
   _____
   b. How do the four inner planets contrast with the outer four? _____
   _____
   c. How does the meaning of the word *compare* help you understand the meaning of the word *contrast*? _____
   _____

Name: _____ Date: _____

FIGURATIVE LANGUAGE – Shades of Meaning

CCSS.ELA-Literacy.L.6.5c: Distinguish among the connotations (associations) of words with similar denotations (definitions) (e.g., stingy, scrimping, economical, unwasteful, thrifty).

Directions: The following words have similar literal meanings (denotations) but different emotional or cultural meanings (connotations). Circle the word that would be best to use in each situation.

1. To describe an admired uncle who is careful with his money:

   a. stingy   b. thrifty   c. miserly   d. penny-pinching

2. To describe a bold fellow student whom you admire:

   a. vain   b. conceited   c. bigheaded   d. confident

3. To describe a quiet baseball player you do not like very much:

   a. timid   b. modest   c. humble   d. unpretentious

4. To describe a sad story you did not enjoy:

   a. poignant   b. depressing   c. moving   d. touching

5. To describe someone who is too energetic:

   a. bouncy   b. lively   c. wired   d. vivacious

6. To describe a foggy morning if you like fog:

   a. misty   b. gloomy   c. bleak   d. overcast

7. To describe a summer day if you like heat:

   a. blistering   b. balmy

   c. sweltering   d. sultry

8. To describe a winter day if you like cold:

   a. invigorating   b. frosty

   c. biting   d. glacial

Answer Keys

READING LITERATURE

Between the Lines (Pg. 1)
1. late afternoon; shadows are deepening.
2. airport, it has a runway
3. frustrated, exasperated or impatient; *exasperated, grimacing, shaking his head*
4. probably rural; barren cliffs, vacant runway, not busy

What Is the Story About? (Pg. 2)
1. man against nature
2. turbulent sea, watched helplessly, ferocious storm
3. storm at sea, dramatic challenge to people on the boat
4. The main character is Daniel. He has to find a way to help. He has to struggle against the elements.

Story plot summaries will vary.

Power Words (Pg. 3)
1. Kuiper Belt; he is interested in science
2. rose up; stuck up, stood, loomed is spooky and ominous—threatening
3. The grave markers are compared to mountains in his grandfather's Chinese ink painting. He is at least part Chinese and he is interested in art. A mechanic might have compared them to pieces of old machinery or equipment
4. ancient, primeval; desolate, dismal; These words carry the feeling of loneliness, timelessness, and loss.

Supporting Roles (Pg. 4)
1. Jason likes Becca, though she may not know it.; winced, felt uncomfortable; It shows Jason is jealous.
2. first love; last sentence
3. second sentence; warm and sunny (shade), probably before or after school or during recess
4. first sentence; Jason. We see the others through his eyes, and we know how he feels. He also has the problem.

Through Arlen's Eyes: Developing a Point of View (Pg. 5)
1. Arlen
2. He is trapped on some kind of ship with two drunk adults who are not his parents.

3. helpless (may vary)
4. Either of the adults would be thinking about his or her anger at the other adult and about the annoying kid.

Answers to essay questions will vary.

READING INFORMATIONAL TEXT

Just the Facts (Pg. 6)
1. clear, blob-like and too small to see with the naked eye
2. lakes, ponds, puddles, creeks; water; Mussels and water fleas eat them. Larger animals eat the mussels and water fleas.
3. eats, eliminates waste, moves, reproduces
4. microscope; can't see with magnifying glass, too small

How Details Add Up: Writing a Summary (Pg. 7)
1. European artists strived for realism.
2. to create an illusion of three-dimensional space
3. to make their portraits more realistic
4. to create realistic textures and effects

Essay answers will vary.

The Clownfish and the Anemone: Using Context Clues (Pg. 8)
1. two organisms need each other to live
2. pulls out, takes
3. Parasites are organisms that use other organisms without giving a benefit in return.
4. Both sides benefit from a relationship. Clownfish and sea anemone benefit each other. Mistletoe benefits and tree is harmed.

One Small Step: What Each Part of a Text Contributes (Pg. 9)
1. Technology was not as advanced as today.
2. Most people did not see the broadcast in color when man stepped on the moon.
3. all eyes were on Neil Armstrong (They were watching the broadcast of the moon landing.)
4. In spite of lower levels of technology, people on Earth were able to watch Armstrong step on the lunar surface.
5. in fact, for example
6. b. sequence

Abuzz With a Point of View: Determining the Author's Purpose (Pg. 10)

1. declining numbers of bumblebees
2. persuade; we must act; find out what you can do
3. Since the 1990s, numbers have declined; some species have almost disappeared; bumblebees pollinate a third of food crops.
4. Study the situation to find out how to help.

A Picture Is Worth a Thousand Words (Pg. 11)

1. A huge boulder in the Mojave Desert; Native Americans/sacred; UFO believers/gathering place; preservationists/restore and protect
2. The scale of the rock, how it stands alone, and its condition
3. Data about size, weight, and composition
4. text: background; picture: appearance and surroundings; chart: size, composition, height, weight; additional media: video of campers, preservationists, or others at the rock, historical photos of people involved, interview with a geologist about why it is there

Prove It! (Pg. 12)

1. Vampire stories provide safe thrills. Students may or may not agree.
2. *Dracula* was published.
3. "Countless"; opinion; probably not; too many published around the world and over too long a time period
4. Answers will vary. Could have included box office receipts for vampire blockbusters
5. Both provide scary situations that are fun. Author could have included quotations from authors, movie makers, or designers of amusement park rides.

Essay question answers will vary.

WRITING—WRITING OPINION PIECES
What I Think: Presenting an Opinion (Pg. 13)

1. School vending machines should sell soda. or School vending machines should not sell soda.
2. Answers will vary.
3. Answers will vary.

Essay question answers will vary.

Nevertheless and Other Joiners (Pg. 14)

Answers will vary, but should use some of the following words to connect ideas: *because, since, yet, in spite of, regardless of, even so, however,* *nevertheless, granted that, as long as, unless, while, with this in mind, due to.*

Dressed to Impress: Using Formal Language (Pg. 15)

Answers will vary, but should use business letter form in the exercise and an informal e-mail style in the challenge.

Clinching the Deal: Writing a Conclusion (Pg. 16)

1. Answers will vary.
2. Answers will vary, but should be a paragraph supporting the idea that summer break is not a good idea.

Challenge essays will vary, but should be supported by research.

WRITING—WRITING INFORMATIVE AND EXPLANATORY TEXTS
Making Ideas Clear: Using Text Structure to Organize an Essay (Pg. 17)

Answers will vary, but both texts should include elements such as headings, charts, maps, or drawings.

Filling in the Blanks: Adding Details and Examples (Pg. 18)

Answers will vary, but should include special terminology related to the sport selected.

Connecting Ideas: Using Transitions (Pg. 19)

Answers will vary, but sentences should include such words as *for example, however, while this may be true, consequently, after, meanwhile, subsequently, nearby, around, even though, similarly, certainly, especially, since, because,* and *therefore.*

Special Words for Special Topics (Pg. 20)

Answers will vary, but should include words specific to the hobby or activity being discussed.

Fitting the Occasion (Pg. 21)

Answers will vary. The following are possible revisions.

1. More than two hundred thousand people gathered on August 28, 1963, for the "March on Washington."
2. There are many ways to create a graph.
3. Animals use natural camouflage to hide from predators.
4. Long ago, people did not know how disease spread.

5. Sound waves travel quickly, but light waves travel even more rapidly. or Sound waves are fast, but light waves are even faster.
6. Scientists possess a great deal of information about volcanoes. or Scientists have learned a great deal about volcanoes.
7. Jane Goodall's work with wild chimpanzees was also interesting.

Sum it Up Beautifully (Pg. 22)
1. Television was invented in the early 1900s and developed into an important medium during the first half of the twentieth century.
2. Sequence
3. Answers will vary.
Challenge answers will vary.

WRITING—WRITING NARRATIVES
The Story Machine (Pg. 23)
Answers will vary.

Observe! (Pg. 24)
Answers will vary.

Moving Right Along (Pg. 25)
1. Suddenly   2. as soon as
3. just in time
4–6. Answers will vary, but should use the word or phrase provided.
Challenge stories will vary.

Make it Vivid (Pg. 26)
Answers will vary.

So What Happened? (Pg. 27)
Answers will vary, but the following are possible:
1. They are rescued.
2. They find an alternate route.
3. His friend gets in trouble anyway.
4. She finds it in her drawer.
5. It is not really his dad.
Stories will vary.

Building a Critique Group (Pg. 28)
Answers will vary, but may include:
   Listen when others are speaking. Take notes. When offering criticism, state what is good about the manuscript first. Be polite. Take turns. Allow all members to speak. Don't defend your work or argue. (You don't have to follow every piece of advice, but you should listen.) Say thank you.

Class magazine responses will vary. Adapt the form to your situation.

WRITING—DRAWING EVIDENCE FROM TEXT
Compare Genres (Pg. 29)
1. "The Last Leaf" is a short story. It is prose, there are more characters, and the old artist sacrifices himself to save the young artist, in the process creating his masterpiece. "One Art" is a poem. It is a strict, extremely difficult form called a Villanelle. In the poem, the narrator is dealing with the probable loss of someone she loves. The masterpiece is the poem itself.
2. In "The Last Leaf" the vine loses its leaves and the old artist loses his life. In "One Art" the speaker loses keys, hours, places, names, and, she fears, a person she loves.
3. In "One Art" the Villanelle form involves a pattern of repeated lines. The word *disaster* tolls through the poem like a bell, along with *master,* which has many meanings. In "The Last Leaf," the window and the vine show up again and again. Art materials and the doctor also make repeat appearances. The doctor says, "she has one chance in ten" and then repeats the phrase improving her chances.
4. In "The Last Leaf" the old artist says the young artist is foolish to believe that she will die when the last leaf falls and pretends not to care, but he cares so much that he gives his life to maintain the illusion for her. In "One Art" the speaker says that the art of losing is not hard to master, but it is so difficult for her to even think of losing this person that the final stanza stutters with pain. She has to force herself to write *disaster*.
Responses to the Frederick Douglass autobiography will vary.

SPEAKING AND LISTENING—DISCUSSIONS
Be Prepared (Pg. 30)
1. You will not feel confident enough to contribute to the discussion and will not be able to understand what people are talking about.
2. Take notes as you read and do research.
3. People express opinions without giving good reasons, and disagreements tend to be more emotional. Nobody is prodded to think in a new direction.
(The robotics discussion is just a suggestion. Feel free to substitute.)

Sharing Ideas (Pg. 31)

Answers will vary, but may include:

Listen. Speak in turn. Acknowledge what previous speakers have said before adding information. Respect other opinions even if you do not agree. Be prepared. Add facts and concrete information such as statistics. Stay on the topic. Speak clearly so others can understand what you are saying. Contribute. Think before you speak.

Questions will vary.

Discussion Reflections (Pg. 32)

Answers will vary.

SPEAKING AND LISTENING—DIVERSE MEDIA AND FORMATS

Experiencing a Great Speech (Pg. 33)

1. It shows the context and reason for the speech—dead soldiers on the battlefield. The written text makes it easier to study the content. The audio presentation adds emotional impact and allows you to experience it as a speech rather than a piece of writing. The introduction adds background. Some students may already know this. Others may have forgotten, so opinions about its helpfulness will vary.

2. Lincoln asserts that the Union that was created by the founding fathers is being tested (by the Civil War). The battleground where the cemetery is located is one proof of that test. He says that people gathered together cannot dedicate or consecrate the cemetery. He supports that by saying that the men who died there have already done that. He says that these men will not have died in vain, then supports that by saying the Union will survive and have a "new birth in freedom" because of their sacrifice.

3. Answers will vary, but may include such observations as: We live in a different time. We know how the war ended. We are not standing in the middle of a field wearing uncomfortable clothes trying to see and hear. Lincoln is not present.

Delivering a Talk (Pg. 34)

Answers will vary.

LANGUAGE—STANDARD ENGLISH AND GRAMMAR USAGE

Three Cases for Pronouns (Pg. 35)

1. Because Gregor Mendel was curious, (he) wondered how pea plants passed traits down to (their) offspring, and so he designed experiments to study (them).

2. In a famous Greek myth, Venus feels sorry for a sculptor (who) has fallen in love with (his) statue, so (she) transforms the sculpture into a real woman.

3. The bus driver ordered Rosa Parks to surrender (her) seat to a white man, but (she) refused to obey (him).

4. When (we) study geography, we use (our) textbooks as well as the Internet and other resources available to (us).

5. (You) are certain to find information about (your) favorite animal online.

6. (I) know (you) have (my) book because (I) gave (it) to (you) when (you) asked (me) to borrow (it).

Challenge: subjective pronoun list: he who, she, we, you, I; Paragraphs will vary.

That's Intense (Pg. 36)

1. If the boys complete that project by (themselves), Principal Hayes (himself) will congratulate them.

2. You two girls must care for that dog (yourselves), because I (myself) am unwilling to assume your responsibilities.

3. We are planning to bring all the food (ourselves), but guests should clean up after (themselves).

4. That report is not going to write (itself), so you (yourself) should start working on it.

Challenge paragraphs will vary.

Do Your Pronouns Agree? (Pg. 37)

1. b. she was supposed to take her seat and start work right away.; she, her

2. a. we always need them in the afternoon.; we; them

3. a. he should sign up early for band.; he

4. a. he was supposed to meet his teacher by the lake.; he, his

Fixing Vague Pronouns (Pg. 38)

Answers may vary according to interpretation of the sentence. Possible answers include:

1. she; When Carly and Maria arrived at the party, Maria hurried into the kitchen to put the drinks in the refrigerator.
2. which; The school rules, which many students resented, prohibited wearing t-shirts with logos.
3. they; As soon as Jason and Michael told their parents about the tournament, the two boys started making plans.
4. he; Mr. DeLawrence had performed on concert stages around the world before Shawn started studying piano with him.
5. he; Sam called Carlos soon after Carlos was hired.
6. she; Claudia bought her sister a tablet computer, but Claudia liked it so much that she kept it for herself and took it to college. (a perverse version to show why the original was ambiguous)

Botched Pronouns (Pg. 39)

1. That lunch is for her and me. (That lunch is for her. That lunch is for me. The pronoun is the object of the preposition *for*.)
2. She and I will accept the award tonight. (Use the subjective form and put yourself last.)
3. Remember, this is between you and me. (between you—between me; objective form)
4. Whoever can hit the ball over the fence is a better batter than I. (*Whoever* is the subjective form. To test, substitute a more familiar subject form such as *he*. He can hit the ball. Note: *I* is correct at the end of this sentence since *am* is understood.)

LANGUAGE—CAPITALIZATION, PUNCTUATION, AND SPELLING

Extra! Extra! (Pg. 40)

1. West Hills Courthouse, which has been protected by legislation for over a decade, could be demolished soon.
2. This winter, the coldest in recent memory, is almost over.
3. The constellation Cassiopeia (named after an ancient queen of Ethiopia) is often easy to spot in the night sky.
4. This week's book fair will (1) raise money for the school library, (2) enable readers to meet their favorite authors, and (3) encourage more students to read for entertainment.
5. My sister—the best in the whole world—has invited me to join her on a backpacking trip this summer.
6. Our new coach—the great Steve Allard—will meet us at the park on Saturday morning.
7. Answers will vary

Spell it Right! (Pg. 41)

1. Answers will vary. May include: makes writing easier to read; builds a reader's confidence in the writer's authority or education; makes writing clearer
2. a. printed dictionary
   b. Internet or digital dictionary
3. It's easier to spot mistakes in work by others.
4. disgize   detane   expecially
5. disguise, detain, especially

LANGUAGE—USING LANGUAGE

Creating Sentence Variety (Pg. 42)

1. b. In Paris on November 21, 1783, a hot-air balloon designed by the Montgolfier brothers carried two pilots aloft.
   c. Designed by the Montgolfier brothers, a hot air balloon carried two pilots aloft in Paris on November 21, 1783.
2. b. On May 29, 1953, Sir Edmund Hillary and Tenzing Norgay became the first climbers to reach the summit of Mt. Everest.
   c. The summit of Mt. Everest was first reached by Sir Edmund Hillary and Tenzing Norgay on May 29, 1953.

Challenge paragraphs will vary.

Formal and Informal Styles (Pg. 43)

Phrases that do not fit the formal style: does other cool stuff, such as like, While this stuff is important,

The spleen filters blood, removing old blood cells from circulation. This organ, which weighs about five ounces, performs other functions such as recycling iron and creating antibodies to fight invading bacteria. While these functions are important, they are not vital. Some people have their spleens removed due to illness or injury. The surgery has some effects, but these effects are not life-threatening.

Informal paragraphs will vary.

What's Does it Mean?: Deciphering Unfamiliar Words (Pg. 44)

1. a. use context clues
   b. look for affixes and roots
   c. look it up in the dictionary
2. a. tree-dwelling   b. creep into, take over
   c. gather   d. very embarrassed
   e. scheming, plotting f. special language
   g. dangerous

Using Context (Pg. 45)

1. c. privacy   2. a. warning
3. a. plentiful   4. c. glowing
5. b. condemned   6. a. undivided
7. b. constant   8. a. an imaginary line

Using Greek and Latin Affixes and Roots to Build Vocabulary (Pg. 46)

1. hearing
2. the sides are of equal length
3. they sail around the world
4. To coordinate means to order two things or groups so they work together. To subordinate means to organize two things or groups so one is below the other or has less power than the other.
5. a change in form
6. living with; two living things that depend on one another for survival
7. air pressure
8. without form
9. dried food; food with the water removed

Challenge answers will vary.

Check it Out: Using the Dictionary (Pg. 27)

1. conVICT (verb): to find guilty
   CONvict (noun): a person who has been found guilty
2. obJECT (verb): to disagree, to protest
   OBject (noun): a thing
3. comPACT (verb): to consolidate or squeeze together
   COMpact: an agreement (the *Mayflower Compact*) or portable case for face powder.
4. conTENT (adj.): satisfied
   CONtent (noun): what is contained or included, substance
5. miNUTE (adj.): extremely small
   MINute (noun): 60 seconds

LANGUAGE—FIGURATIVE LANGUAGE
It's a Figure of Speech: Personification (Pg. 48)

1. a. A winter storm is moving into town.
   b. a person, probably a man
   c. irascible
   d. a cloak (heavy cape)
   e. chased the last warm day (implied, like a pretty girl) out of town
2. a. The computer isn't working right after a new hardware installation.
   b. stubbornly
   c. no
   d. displayed error messages and/or made its error sound; would not turn on
   e. a person
3. Answers will vary.

Words That Belong Together (Pg. 49)

1. a. cause
   b. They are opposites and work together to show the relationship between two events. An effect cannot exist without a cause. If something just happens, it isn't an effect.
2. a. part
   b. There cannot be a part without a whole. The word *part* implies there are additional components or a larger context.
3. a. planets in our solar system
   b. The word *category* means a group or class and implies that it contains items. If it did not, it would be an item, not a category.
4. a. They are all terrestrial, or rocky.
   b. The outer four are different because they are larger and composed of gas.
   c. They are opposites, but related. *Compare* emphasizes similarities, while *contrast* emphasizes differences.

Shades of Meaning (Pg. 50)

1. b. thrifty   2. d. confident
3. a. timid   4. b. depressing
5. c. wired   6. a. misty
7. b. balmy   8. a. invigorating